left behind

a collection of dark poetry

left behind
a collection of dark poetry

scott swenson

Published by Scott Swenson
2016

First Printing: 2016

ISBN 978-1-365-32871-8

Scott Swenson
PO Box 9882
Tampa, Florida 33674

www.ScottSwenson.com

Ordering Information:

Special discounts are available on quantity purchases by corpora-
tions, associations, educators, and others. For details, contact the
publisher at the above listed address.

U.S. trade bookstores and wholesalers: Please contact scott swen-
son via email scottswenson63@gmail.com

an explanation

The poetry in this book was inspired by the
stories, locations and characters from

THE VAULT OF SOULS

an interactive performance art event with a dark and
sinister twist. These live evenings of elegant fear first took
place in October of 2015 at
The Vault, 611 North Franklin Street, Tampa,Florida.
This collection was created for the 2016 season and is a
follow up to the first book,

"souls: a collection of dark poetry"

For more information about "The Vault of Souls" please
visit www.ElegantFear.com

contents

Left Behind

Another year
The vault descends
How deep it goes
That all depends
On the whispers and echoes
And where they lead
Your hunger for knowledge
And where you feed
More secrets to learn
More answers to find
Will you be a resident
Or just left behind

Griffin's Dream

I'm looking towards the horizon
For our bank and for our city
I see an opportunity
For both profit and for pity

I'll create a place for sinners
Who need to cleanse their vital force
A paranormal halfway house
That helps correct their course

When clients are concerned
About what their afterlife will be
I'll offer an alternative
For those who pay the fee

Who knows more about security
Than our esteemed and honored bank
For spiritual protection
It is Griffin they will thank

This altruistic venture
We'll surpass our business goals
May I introduce to you
The one and only Vault of Souls

Clown

With trembling hand a single tear is placed
Black pigment at the corner of his eye
A permanent mark without the salty taste
Painted on for he can no longer cry

A downward curve is drawn upon his face
The frown his broken heart demands to show
Triangles around his eyes are now in place
As he grieves for those he lost somewhere below

His visage is finished for the waiting crowd
The powder and the brushes put aside
Escaping thoughts of cries he heard out loud
The stage is now his safest place to hide

Music Box Beauty

One single point
Supports the elegance and grace
Otherworldly balance
Iron form and porcelain face

Costumes and makeup
Memories of a life in the light
Bandages and bleeding toes
Realities only seen by night

Music box beauty
Sugar plum and dying swan
Now just an echo
But the ballerina dances on

Vaporous Hints

For decades this room has been filled with those who hope
to cheat their fate
Some did it for money, some did it for love, just as many
did it for hate
These walls have soaked up memories as past guests have
milled about
But when the limit is reached, some memories leak out

As the sun sets, twilight approaches and darkness fills
the spaces
More sensitive guests or innocent souls may catch glimpses
of human faces
These snippets of ghosts or partial spirits may peer in from
the other side
But being only memories, confused, they will
retreat and hide

Please do not try to assist them it will only make the
confusion worse
They are vaporous hints from times gone by, a swirling
ghostly curse
Most of them are just passing thoughts, they don't even
know their name
But pity these misguided wisps, for in the future
you may be the same

The Roadster

Want to go for a ride? I'll put down the top
This roadster is really a Breezer

My baby doll is the cat's meow
I got it just to please her

Hold on tight, I'm flooring it now
My baby would scream with joy

Well not anymore since I bumped her off
She was cheating with another boy

I followed her home and that's when I saw
She was grinding her chassis on you

Yes I know who you are, you philandering oaf
And I know just what to do

We'll drive off the pier and into the drink
Yes, I have taken an oath

To finish the chapter of my broken heart
By crashing and ending us both

I want you to know, before we race off
The dock and I take your life

That I have delivered a handwritten note
Explaining this all to your wife

The Historian

He's never entered the world below, perhaps he never will
He works to understand it though, his file cases filled
Document one
The daughter and son
Document two
Discovering who
Document three
A receipt for a fee
Document four
Another closed door
His work is all he has in life, a focus without end
He has no time to take a wife, confidante or friend
Document five
She's still alive
Document six
A dominatrix
Document seven
She was only eleven
Document eight
An unfortunate fate
The fuse of time is burning fast, he works as hard as he can
His next find may be his last, he is only a single man
Document nine
The Atlantic Coast Line
Document ten
The reflection of men
Document eleven
No chance at Heaven
Document twelve

Remains on the shelves

The Mask

I will be safe
As long as I wear the mask
It hides my face
So no ancestor will ask
To follow me home
Because they know my voice
I'll follow the rules
I really have no choice
If I am to return
To the place above the ground
And live my life
Without the echoing sound
Of an antique clock
With a ringing spectral chime
I could be possessed
By a precursor out of time
So I must wear the mask
And be silent as a stone
It will help guarantee
That I will leave this place alone

The Book Keeper

The book is out and open
A space to sign your name
He stands there watching silently
For everyone its the same

You document your presence
Your visit to the vault
Your character is scrutinized
Dismissal is your fault

Before you meet the spirits
You must pass his critical eye
He is now the gatekeeper
Only the worthy will get by

His voice has long been silenced
His lips forever sealed
This is the price he paid
For the power that he wields

He remembers every visitor
He studies every face
He has tracked each resident
In this dark confining place

Dearest Lucy

I know she lives eternally but my heart still is broken
So many years since we saw her face or heard a word she's spoken

We tried so hard to join her but were blocked at every turn
Her Mother passed with ignorance but I was left to learn

That Lucy was surrounded by the spirits and the damned
This information vexed me so I took a final stand

I consorted with the orators for those who had no voice
The vision-gifted Mystics were my conspirators of choice

The goal was clearly stated it was to break into the vault
Where her spirit was imprisoned, guarded to a fault

You may think I'd want to free her, but that was not the case
I just wanted to hold her or simply see her face

I stood inside the circle with the Mystics all around
They chanted in a single voice I was caught up in the sound

The deadly herbs they gave me made the room begin to whirl
But soon there was a tunnel of light and I could see my little girl

I tried to run and sweep her up but my legs and feet had froze
When I was able to regain myself the tunnel began to close

I dove into the vortex as I heard the Mystics shout
I was halfway down the corridor, I knew there was no way out

The iris portal closing just as Lucy turned in fear
Her eye caught mine and mine caught hers, we shared a
single tear

I never held my little girl and I am forever trapped between
The world of the living and place where specters dream

Dearest Lucy is protected by the walls and earth above
And she will live eternally enveloped in my love

Buckshot in the Glass

We thought is was an easy heist
No one cared about Mob dough
The inside man would be in place
How much easier could it go?

No lock on the door and no alarm was set
It was a straight shot to the cash
Then out of the vault came three armed men
We heard a noise and saw a flash

Jimmy went down in a flutter of red
I tried to reach for my gun
But 5 more shotgun blasts rang out
We all fell and the caper was done

The thing we didn't consider
Or honestly even think through,
The bank may not care about Capone's cash
But Mr. Capone and his associates do

The buckshot is still scattered through the glass
Where the night teller used to be
The memory is trapped in the private safe
Just like the souls of my gang and me

finding a descendant

when I was a child
I knew daddy's smell
it was part what he wore
but his own scent as well

then i went to church
to learn of God's goal
i thought daddy's aroma
might be that of his soul

i've missed that perfume
for so many years
i smell it tonight and
it brings happy tears

i know you aren't daddy
but you do have his voice
and also his scent
so i've made the choice

to never again
live without his bouquet
so i will live in your shadows
till your very last day

he buried his love

he buried his love and coldly locked the door
the forbidden secret was safe and never found
still hearing echoed curses from below
once joyful, that voice became a dreadful sound

his wife was deposited in the same gilded crypt
but her remains were more grandly displayed
the candles cast light over granite walls
but soon darkness fell where the coffin was laid

lightless, silent spirits found each other
united by the love for the same man
each realized the other had been wronged
vengeance became their eternally focussed plan

they knew they could not reach to him in life
he needed to be close to death it seems
the lover and wife knew when they could attack
as the man slept they crept into his dreams

night after night as he prepared for sleep
they searched for all the horror they could find
without him suspecting their vindictive plot
they wove it deeply into his troubled mind

it came to pass the man avoided sleep
day after day he fought to stay awake
eventually his battle had to reach an end
his torn and addled brain began to break

today he lives a silent life alone
restrained and buckled firmly to his bed
never knowing who had dealt his fate
lover and wife, revenge came from the dead

Waiting for the Fall

Hanging by a strand of hair
A blade, suspended overhead
Sitting on a wooden chair
Staring up, already dead

Eager face, translucent eyes
Fixated on the swinging knife
This echoed spirit is very wise
There is no threat or endangered life

So why would she endure this trial
Sitting still against the wall
Anticipation, fervent smile
Waiting for the knife to fall

Since she passed she hasn't aged
Expectation is her only friend
She must keep her mind engaged
For in her world, time has no end

Reflection

I see my reflection
I feel the rejection
I loved you more than you hated me

Seeing my face
Put my feelings in place
Whatever those feelings may be

I knew in my head
You wanted me dead
But my heart was holding me fast

I wanted to leave
Before you could grieve
Alas, the tragic play had been cast

Oh yes I was wise
As you planned my demise
And I knew of your many secret loves

So on the night of my death
When you snuffed out my breath
While wearing your black leather gloves

I made a pact
From beyond I would act
My memory you never could flee

Now whenever you pass
A mirror of glass
It is my face you forever will see

still without a sound

take a walk through the mounds
each one holds the remains of the past
buried beneath the ground
medicine woman spells were cast
still without a sound
stones in place and holding fast
some things lost can not be found
bodies decay but memories last

The Marble and The Button

I found a marble and a button on the floor beside my bed
The marble was made of agate, the button was bright red

I've never played with marbles and this button isn't mine
It looks like it was quickly stitched with a length of yellow twine

I have no fear of these objects, they do not pose a threat
So why, when I look at them, do I tremble and I sweat?

Then I look up at the painting hanging on my wall
Its been there since I was young, I hardly notice it at all

But as I look more closely there are children on the ground
Playing a game of marbles just like the one I found

The shooter is bent over and ready to take his shot
But his hand is empty, what was once painted there is not

I quickly scan the painting for a button that is missing
I see the ice cream vendor and the couple that is kissing

I keep dissecting every inch of this old painting of a park
But I find no missing button, perhaps the room's too dark

So I flip on the table lamp and turn back to the wall and see
Something that I'd missed before, a clown behind a tree

I had never seen him painted there, almost hiding on his own
His face was painted sternly, a completely different tone

Down the front of his costume was a short length of yellow twine
And carved into the bark of the tree was a single word...mine

several little locks

got a secret
hide it away
put it in a box
safe behind
the vaulted door
and several little locks
documents
love letters
words that no one sees
trapped in time
in the dark
until someone finds the keys
open the box
release the past
buried words uncovered
the question is
is it safe
for the covert to be discovered
mysteries
corrupted thoughts
may have been hidden for a purpose
what will happen
when these words
are brought back to the surface
was it right
for missives
to be hidden from the eyes of man
or is the evil
now unlocked
part of a grander plan
the time has come
release the words
now speak the incantation
language virus
now begins
a wicked infestation

A Businessman Out in the Sun

Mr Johnson, Mr. Black
Back up north I have a knack
Of changing my name and my face

But at the end of the line
My name is just mine
No one knows who I am in this place

Mr. Smith, Mr. Grey
When I'm here by the bay
I'm a tourist instead of a thug

A fine place to stash
My ill-gotten cash
In a bank, not under the rug

Mr. Jones, Mr. White
There is no need to fight
Instead I've decided to run

On the Florida shore
I'm no less and no more
Than a businessman out in the sun

the puddle

seeping up through the cracks
the puddle expands
on the concrete floor
over hourglass sands
sweat from the workers
mud from the street
this is the border
where then and now meet
dripping from walls
or the ghosts of the sea
looking down for my reflection
but that face isn't me
bloated and blue
this spirit has drowned
in this thin film of water
here on the ground
behind him are fathoms
no one can remember
shipwrecks and bridges
the extinguished ember
of lives lost and suspended
in the saline deep
floating forever
in unending sleep
its the liquid of knowledge
so drink from it's cup
for the iris will close
when the puddle dries up

She Was My Daughter

She was my daughter
       But then they took her to this place
I need to find her
       But the darkness hides her face
My heart still loves her
       Though my body rots away
Until I see her
       My eternal soul will stay
Please help me find her
       So I can finally be at rest
I must take her
       Or at least I'll do my best
To help release her
       From this prison of eternal sleep
If I can't save her
       I will forever weep

The Dentist

Pain free extraction
Grinding tooth action
Researching decay

Inserting fillings
In those who are willing
But the Doctor has now gone astray

This demented physician
Has changed his mission
Some think he's just insane

Now his game
His target and aim
Is maximizing pain

When he chose
To leave nerves exposed
Some thought it was by mistake

No, now his goal
Is to cleanse the soul
With excruciating torment and ache

This Dentist believes
That when he relieves
He weakens the human race

So the pain he dispenses
Builds stronger defenses
But mangles the patient's face

Sobbing and screams
Are filling his dreams
He's a monster who generates fear

But he goes to great lengths
To build up our strengths
With the falling of each single tear

The Parlor

The smell of old pillows
Photos on the table
Piano in the corner
She plays it when she's able

Fire on the hearth
Doilies on the chair
Working stereopticon
Silver comb for her hair

This room has been her haven
Sometimes laughter, sometimes tears
Can't remember ever leaving
Not in many years

This parlor is the only place
For her to lay her head
She doesn't seem to realize
That she's already dead

She can't see the visitors
But some can hear her voice
She didn't get to make one
But if she had a choice

Of where to spend eternity
This is where she'd stay
Rocking in her rocking chair
Through her eternal day

Transition

When the organ music plays
It signals end of days
There are oh so many ways
To pass from one world to the next

For many its the goal
To not travel "down the hole"
So they protect their soul
With platitudes and text

But here, there is no worry
To suffer fire and furry
Relax, there is no hurry
We're in control of this endeavor

No talismans or salt
To purge you of your fault
Welcome to The Vault
You'll be with us forever

words form a web

words form a web that tangles and twists
a net to support what is real
a series of stories and scribbles and lists
some expose and some hide what they feel
not all the stories are clearly in view
some are hidden away
connecting ideas may reveal something new
is it truth or a lie? whose to say
explore the dark corners and stay acutely aware
engage with your heart and your mind
the story you leave with, the story you share
is all based on the secrets you find

From the Bathtub to the Bar Room

From the bathtub to the bar room
Let the Devil's nectar flow
Drink the liquor and the specters
Will line up for the show
Demon rum will tear down borders
Bringing vision to the blind
Seek salvation in the bottle
It will open up your mind
The green fairy dances lightly
Through the thoughts of those enlightened
But when she's followed down the hole
The uninspired become frightened
Let the coffin varnish lead you
Stamp your ticket board the ship
Comfort spirits are your pilots
On this paranormal trip
You must trust the apparitions
From the moment you embark
Or you will be abandoned
Lost and lonely in the dark

The Iron Shadow

A shadow is cast from the man in charge
silent but ever near
As the sun goes down the darkness grows large
protecting the boss from fear

It has no name, no voice, no face
in a crowd it stands alone
This pinstriped monolith fills the space
unmovable as stone

But does the dark contour ever hope
for a moment in the sun?
And if it treads this slippery slope
will its power be undone?

This Iron shadow must be ever steady
in order to play its part
Its muscles tense and always ready
with a black and stone cold heart

Single Thread

She enters the room and silently rises
The air supports her form
She twists and turns from a single thread
Movement outside the norm

Dancing in dimensions above the floor
The personification of grace
Her life unwinds in the empty world
Spirit dangling in vacant space

Freedom personified she has no ties
A memory suspended
When she returns to solid ground
Her blissful dream has ended

The Clearing

The concrete floor is filled with gouges and stains
This building's age is showing
Overhead there are tangled rafters and pipes
Silhouetted in blue light glowing
Strangers come to share their observations and thoughts
Tales of wrong and right
Under a sky of dangling electrical stars
Like natives in the night
These adventure seeking travelers are drawn together
Almost against their will
To feel the warmth of common experiences
To chase away the chill
The Readers, like modern day Shamans share their words
With those so inclined
To believe in the those things that can not be seen or heard
Existing only in the mind
The stories told here will echo through this empty place
But may not make a sound
Only those gathered here tonight will understand
That this is hallowed ground

The End of Night

The candles snuffed, white smoke unwinds the dark
The strings are still and silence settles in
The guests are gone but still retain the spark
Of elegant fear and playfully shrouded sin

The building creaks and sighs in dark relief
The moonlight streams metered paths across the floor
Time has played the party's master thief
And emptiness returns, just like before

This is when, from shadows, spirits creep
The specters study the aftermath to learn
Of what the guests will see when home they sleep
And how to nurture dread when they return